Stopwatch books in hardback

Apple tree
Butterfly and caterpillar
Chicken and egg
Conker
Dandelion
Dragonfly
Earwig
Fly
Honeybee
House mouse

Ladybird
Mosquito
Moth
Mushroom
Newt
Potato
Stickleback
Strawberry
Tadpole and frog
Tomato

First paperback edition 1992

Reprinted 1993

First published 1984 in hardback by
A & C Black (Publishers) Limited
35 Bedford Row, London WC1R 4JH

ISBN 0–7136–3621–1

A CIP catalogue record for this book
is available from the British Library.

Acknowledgements
The artwork is by B. L. Kearley Ltd

Filmset by August Filmsetting, Haydock, St Helens
Printed in Belgium by Proost International Book Production

Tadpole and frog

Christine Back
Photographs by Barrie Watts

Adam and Charles Black · London

Here is some frog-spawn.

Have you ever looked at a pond or a ditch and found some frog-spawn?

You can see some frog-spawn in the photograph. Look at the black dots in the frog-spawn. The dots are frog's eggs. Some of these eggs will turn into young frogs, like this one.

This book tells you how the eggs turn into young frogs.

Here is a male frog and a female frog.
The female frog is laying her eggs.

In spring, frogs lay their eggs in ponds and ditches.
Look at the photograph. The male frog is on top of the
female frog. He is waiting for her to lay some eggs.

The female frog lays hundreds of eggs in the water.
The male frog covers the eggs with liquid from his body.

The eggs sink to the bottom of the pond. Then the frogs
swim away. They do not stay to look after their eggs.

Each egg is inside a ball of jelly.

Here is an egg inside its jelly-ball.

In this photograph the jelly-ball is shown very large.
In real life, it is about as big as a pea.

The jelly-balls stick together. We call them frog-spawn.
They float to the top of the pond. The water is warmer
at the top of the pond. This helps the eggs to grow.
Soon the eggs start to change shape. The outside of
each egg begins to look bumpy.

The eggs change into tadpoles.

The eggs change shape very quickly.
After four days, they look like this.

After seven days, the eggs have almost turned into
tadpoles. Look at the big photograph. Can you see the
tadpole's head and tail?

The tadpoles come out of the jelly-balls.

After ten days, the tadpoles are ready to come out of the jelly-balls. The jelly gets softer and the tadpoles wriggle out, like this.

Look at the big photograph. The tadpoles stay together. They rest near the jelly, or on plants.

The tadpoles can breathe underwater.

Each tadpole breathes through feathery gills
on the outside of its body. Look at the photograph.
Can you see the tadpole's gills?

Here is a drawing of a tadpole with gills.

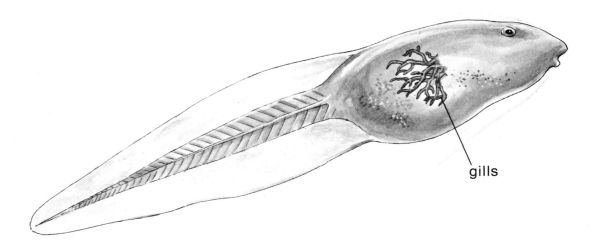

gills

The tadpole swims by wiggling its tail. It eats tiny
plants which grow in the water.

The tadpole grows back legs.

After five weeks, the tadpole has grown back legs. Its outside gills have disappeared. The tadpole can still breathe underwater. Now it breathes through gills which are inside its body.

The tiny tadpoles have many enemies.

This tadpole is being attacked by a beetle larva. Lots of tadpoles are eaten by other animals.

Now the tadpole cannot breathe underwater.

After about six weeks, the tadpole stops using its gills.
The tadpole grows lungs and breathes air like we do.
This means that the tadpole has to come to the top of
the water to breathe.

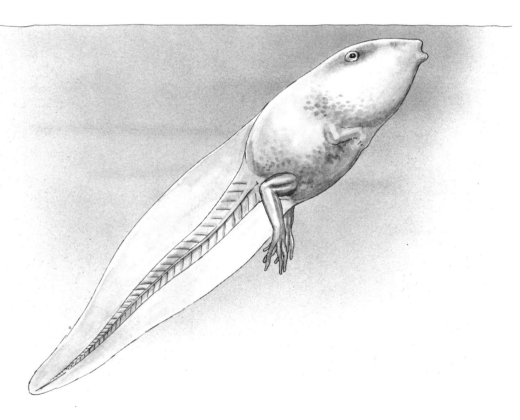

Soon the tadpole grows front legs. Look at the
photograph. This tadpole is ten weeks old.

The tadpole eats small animals.

The tadpole starts to eat small animals
which live in the water.

Look at the drawing.

Can you see that the tadpole's tail is getting shorter?
Soon the tadpole begins to look more like a frog.
Look at the photograph. This tadpole is twelve weeks old.

The tadpole has turned into a frog.
It lives on land.

After fifteen weeks, the tadpole has turned into
a tiny frog.

The frog leaves the water and lives on land.
It uses its strong back legs to jump from place to place.
But the frog still goes back to the pond for a swim.

The tiny frog grows up.

Soon the frog moves away from the pond. The frog lives in damp places and it eats insects, beetles and worms.

The frog slowly grows up to look like its mother or father. Look at the photograph. This female frog is a year old. Next spring, the frog will go to a pond and lay some eggs, like these.

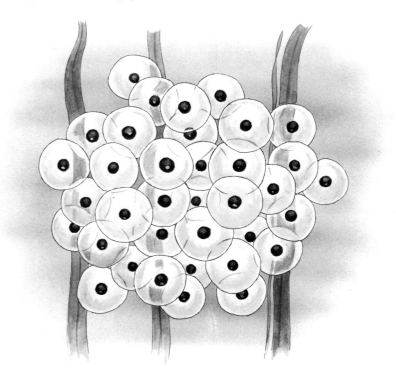

What do you think will happen to the eggs?

Do you remember how frogs' eggs turn into young frogs?
See if you can tell the story in your own words.
You can use these pictures to help you.

Index

This index will help you to find some of the important words in the book

3

6

If you want to watch tadpoles grow, try keeping them in a bowl.
But don't forget to put in a stone which sticks out of the water.